Successful Study:
A Practical Way to Get a Good Degree

edited by

Matt Hector-Taylor
and
Marie Bonsall

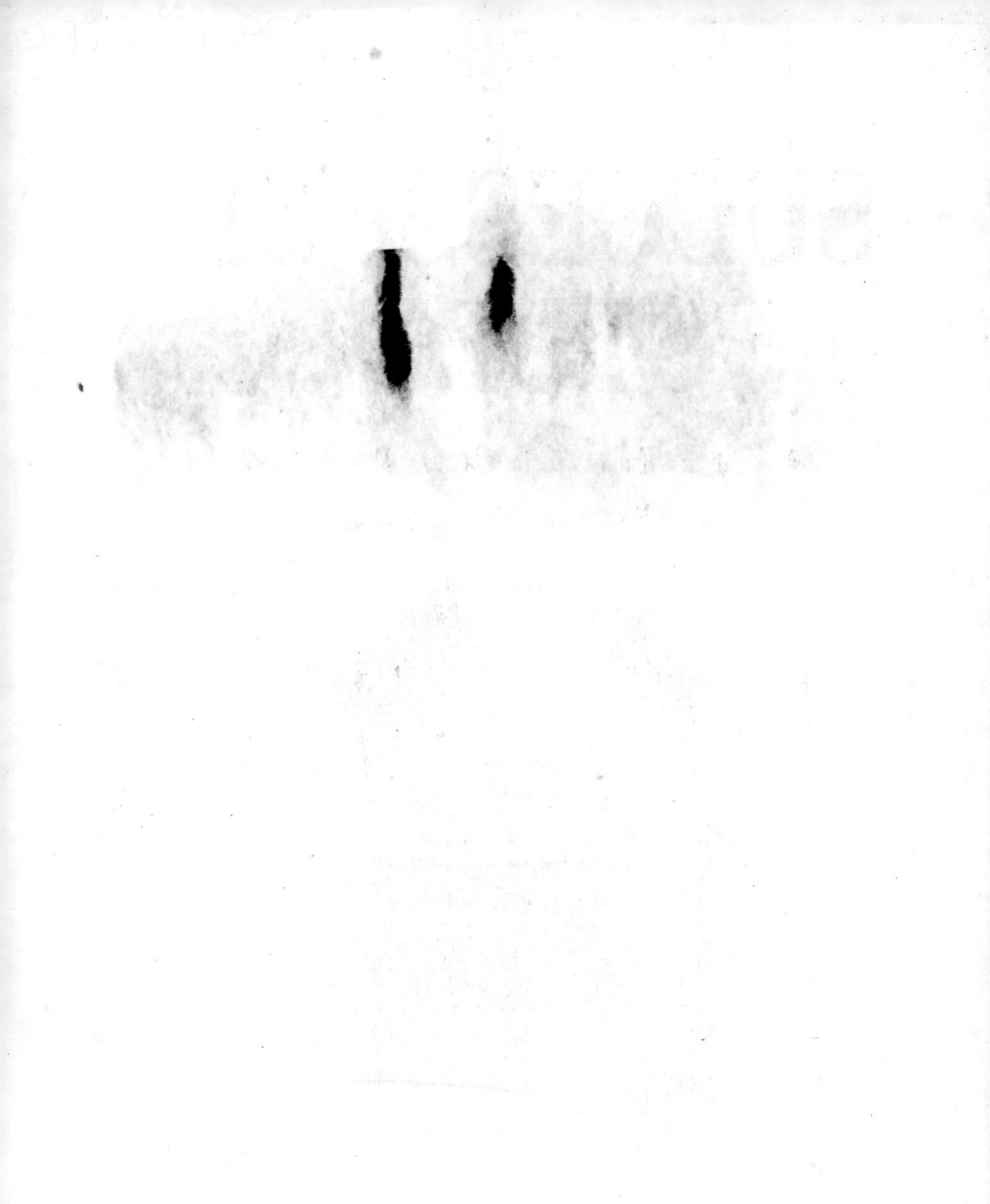

SUCCESSFUL STUDY

A Practical Way to Get a Good Degree

Edited by
**Matt Hector-Taylor
and Marie Bonsall**

The **Hallamshire** Press
1993

Copyright © 1993 The University of Sheffield

Published by The Hallamshire Press
The Hallamshire Press is an imprint of
Interleaf Productions Limited
Exchange Works
Sidney Street
Sheffield S1 3QF
England

Typeset by Interleaf Productions Limited
and
Printed in Great Britain
by
The Cromwell Press
Wiltshire.

British Library Cataloguing in Publication Data

Successful Study:Practical Way to Get a Good Degree
  I. Hector-Taylor, Matt II. Bonsall, Marie
  378.1

ISBN 1-874718-30-X

CONTENTS

Acknowledgements   6

Preface   7

1 Looking at Learning   9

2 Successful Study   25

3 Wrestling with Writing   51

4 Grappling with Group Work   65

5 Simple Solutions   75

6 Painless Presentations   85

ACKNOWLEDGEMENTS

THE EDITORS would like to acknowledge the preparatory work of Edward Buck and Veronica Locatelli for the section *Simple Solutions*, Cara for *Wrestling with Writing* and Sasha Finn for *Successful Study*.

PREFACE

THIS BOOK evolved from *Painless Presentations*, which was the first section to be written. Its aim was to offer tips and advice to students who were required to give presentations as part of their course. Students found this guidance useful, and so we have now prepared similar guidance for a range of activities which students will encounter during their time in Higher Education.

Successful Study: A Practical Way to Get a Good Degree consists of six sections. The emphasis in each section, and in the book as a whole, is on giving common-sense advice and tips that are relevant to studying in Higher Education, and that give you a practical way to get a good degree. The advice is basic, but we hope it will provide you with a suitable starting point for developing your own approach to learning.

'Looking at Learning' (Section 1) aims to help you identify your learning style and provides techniques to help you improve and develop it.

'Successful Study' (Section 2) provides advice on a wide range of general study activities. These include personal time management, using the library, note taking, and assessment.

'Wrestling with Writing' (Section 3) gives more detailed guidance on an extremely important part of student life — writing. It breaks down writing for essays, reports and projects into discrete stages and outlines the action you can take at each stage.

'Grappling with Group Work' (Section 4) was written to help students who were required to work in groups as part of their course — for example, on group projects. It gives information on how groups work, roles in groups, and features of successful groups. It also gives an example of a typical student group task.

Successful Study

'Simple Solutions' (Section 5) addresses the skill of problem solving. In many courses you may be required to apply theoretical knowledge to solve a practical problem. 'Simple Solutions' provides a model for problem solving and gives an example of the problem-solving process.

'Painless Presentations' (Section 6) includes information on structuring presentations, delivery, visual aids, and question handling.

1 LOOKING AT LEARNING

LEARNING underlies many of the activities which we are all involved in as part of our daily lives. For example, taking up a new hobby, learning to drive a car, or studying for a qualification. However, typically we have very little awareness of the factors which determine why we learn in the way that we do.

In Higher Education, you will be expected to take responsibility for your own learning. Your lecturers and tutors will provide you with the general framework for the subject area through material presented in lectures, tutorials, practicals and project work. They may also support you in your learning by recommending reading and commenting on your performance and progress. However, ultimately your success depends on you knowing how to make the most of the learning opportunities that you are presented with.

Different people learn best in different situations. This can depend on their personality, their previous learning experiences, their purpose for learning, their motivation and the demands of the learning task. If you are to be successful, it is essential that you can identify and optimise the situations in which you learn best early on. It is also important that you try to broaden your learning style so that you can learn efficiently and effectively in a wider range of situations.

CONTENTS

This section aims to help you identify your learning style by asking you to think about how you behave and feel in different learning situations. It then provides techniques to help you improve and develop your learning style so that you are able to learn effectively in a wider range of learning situations.

HOW TO USE 'LOOKING AT LEARNING'

It is advisable to read this chapter and identify your learning style before you read other sections in this book. It will help determine your starting point and it will give you a better idea of the sort of skills you still need to develop. Sections in the remainder of this book will provide advice and techniques to help you develop these skills.

The diagram opposite illustrates a simple model of learning. For convenience, learning is split into two distinct stages: (1) gathering information; and (2) cognitively processing the information.

1. GATHERING INFORMATION

At the first stage, individuals use their listening skills, their comprehension skills, their questioning skills, their reading skills, and their communication skills to gather information from the external world. Theories of learning suggest that most individuals have preferred ways of gathering information from the situations that they encounter. For example, in tutorials some students prefer to sit back and listen, whereas others prefer to get actively involved in the discussion and debate. This may depend on individuals' particular skills, i.e. listening, questioning, etc. It may also depend on their personality and their previous learning experiences, i.e. were they expected to participate in class discussion at school, or did the teacher do all the talking while they just sat and listened?

The next section is designed to help you establish your preferred way of gathering information.

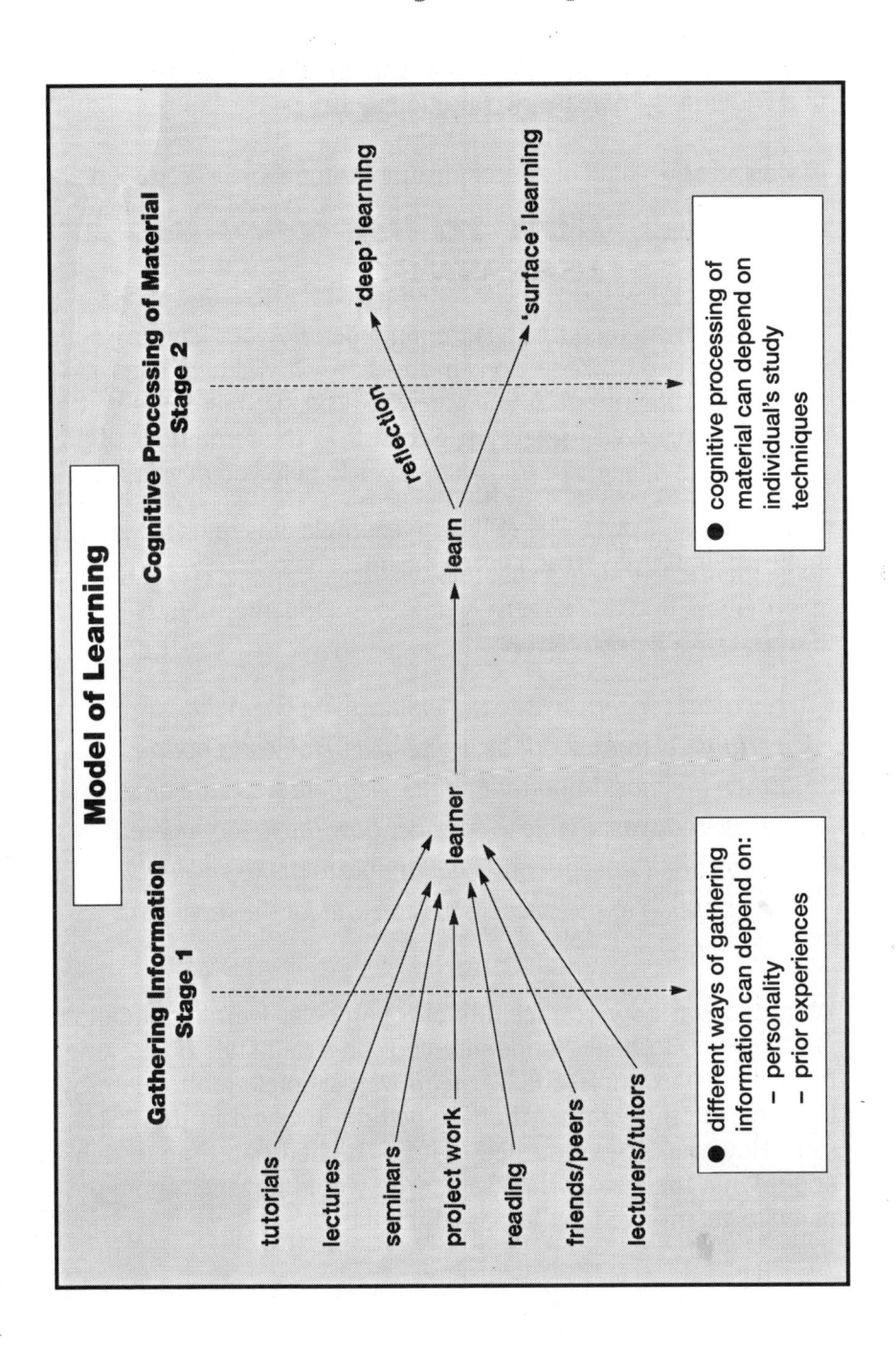

1. Looking at Learning

Model of Learning

Gathering Information — Stage 1

- tutorials
- lectures
- seminars
- project work
- reading
- friends/peers
- lecturers/tutors

→ learner

- different ways of gathering information can depend on:
  - personality
  - prior experiences

Cognitive Processing of Material — Stage 2

learner → learn → reflection → 'deep' learning / 'surface' learning

- cognitive processing of material can depend on individual's study techniques

HOW DO YOU GATHER INFORMATION?

Exercise: Think of a recent learning situation, i.e. lecture, practical class, private study, or group work exercise. Consider your answers to the following questions:

- ▼ What did you like about it?
- ▼ What did you dislike about it?
- ▼ How did you feel about learning in this situation?
- ▼ Why was this so?

Discuss your answers with friends to see how their likes/dislikes differ from your own. The following example illustrates the sort of thing you might say in answer to the questions.

Example comment

My main concern was to understand and grasp the conceptual framework by listening carefully and noting down the most important points. As there was little time to reflect, I was unable to consider how the theory related to practice. Consequently, I felt unable to make a valuable contribution to the class discussion and for the most part I remained quiet.

Writing down how you feel about a particular learning situation will help you to begin to identify your preferred style of learning. In the above example, the learner obviously preferred to learn by listening to others rather than by getting involved in the discussion. However, s/he indicated that if s/he had had time to think about what the lecturer had said, s/he would have felt more prepared to get involved in the class discussion.

1. Looking at Learning

Some writers[1] suggest that there are four basic learning styles. Read the following descriptions and try and decide which one describes your preferred style of learning most closely. Once you have identified your learning style, techniques will be suggested to help you improve and extend it.

THE ACTIVIST

The activist

- ▼ Enjoys new experiences and challenges.
- ▼ Thrives best in situations where s/he can be involved in a constantly changing range of activities.
- ▼ Enjoys being at the centre of attention, whether chairing discussions or giving a presentation.
- ▼ Benefits from the opportunity to develop ideas through discussion and interaction with others.

The Activist

---

1. P. Honey and A. Mumford, *Using your Learning Styles* (Maidenhead: Pete Honey Publications, 1986).

Successful Study

The activist is likely to learn most effectively through group work, discussions, seminars, programmes of short activities, workshops, and study networks.

The activist

- ▼ Dislikes taking a passive role in learning.
- ▼ Does not enjoy tightly constrained tasks, or tasks where s/he has to assimilate and interpret a lot of complex information.
- ▼ Prefers to work with others rather than on his/her own.

The activist is likely to learn least effectively from lectures, lab classes (where the experimental method is prescribed) and reading, writing and thinking on his/her own.

THE REFLECTOR

The reflector

- ▼ Likes the opportunity to think, and mull over, all the implications of what s/he hears or reads before making a decision.
- ▼ Prefers to take a back seat in discussions.
- ▼ Learns from listening to, and observing, others rather than contributing him/herself.
- ▼ Enjoys the opportunity to work independently.
- ▼ Prefers to produce well-considered and thorough work, rather than taking short cuts to meet deadlines.

The reflector is likely to learn most effectively through individual project work, lectures and independent study.

1. Looking at Learning

The Reflector

The reflector

▼ Dislikes being forced to contribute to a discussion without carefully considering all the evidence first.

▼ Does not enjoy being rushed from one activity to another.

▼ Worries if deadlines force him/her to produce work without careful consideration and thought.

The reflector is likely to learn least effectively from spontaneous activity which does not allow time for careful planning and preparation, i.e. role plays and spontaneous group discussion.

THE THEORIST

The theorist

▼ Learns most effectively when dealing with models and theories.

▼ Enjoys exploring connections between ideas, issues and concepts.

Successful Study

- ▼ Is concerned to ensure that arguments and methodologies underpinning theories are rational and logical.
- ▼ Thrives on understanding and participating in complex situations.
- ▼ Likes a clear and definite purpose for his/her work.

The theorist is likely to learn most effectively through problem classes, discussing and questioning theory with peers and tutors, or reading and evaluating books and articles.

The Theorist

The theorist

- ▼ Dislikes being involved in unstructured situations with no obvious theoretical or conceptual framework.
- ▼ Is highly suspicious of subject material without a sound methodological base.
- ▼ Is likely to be more comfortable with objective facts, and less comfortable with subjective emotions and feelings.

1. Looking at Learning

The theorist is likely to learn least effectively from open-ended questions, explorative project work, skills training, etc.

THE PRAGMATIST

The pragmatist

- ▼ Enjoys seeing how theory relates to practice.
- ▼ Enjoys learning practical techniques which may be relevant to his/her subject area and future employment.
- ▼ Likes to reinforce what s/he has learnt through practical problem solving.
- ▼ Prefers to focus on practical rather than theoretical issues.
- ▼ Likes clear guidelines to work to.

The Pragmatist

Successful Study

The pragmatist is likely to learn most effectively through work-based projects, work experience, practical problem solving, lab experiments, etc.

The pragmatist

▼ Dislikes learning situations where the material is too theoretically based.

▼ Dislikes learning situations where s/he can not see the practical application, or relevance of the material covered.

The pragmatist is likely to learn least effectively from theoretical discussion, debate, etc.

Although you may recognise various aspects of yourself in all of the descriptions, there will probably be one which you feel describes you more closely than all of the others. This is your preferred learning style, and it gives you an indication of the situations in which you are likely to learn most/least effectively.

Your learning style has probably developed as a result of your particular skills and the ways in which you have learnt to learn in the past. Although you may always feel most comfortable learning in this way, there is nothing to stop you developing new skills and learning to learn in different ways. In fact, you are more likely to be successful, and to get the most out of your career, if you can learn effectively from the full range of situations that you encounter. You could try any of the following techniques to help you develop skills and learn to learn in new ways. Alternatively, you may have your own ideas. You should aim to practise your new techniques as often as possible. Remember, it won't be easy at first, and not all of the techniques will necessarily suit you. Keep experimenting until you find one which does, and persevere with it until it becomes second nature.

1. Looking at Learning

SUGGESTED TECHNIQUES FOR DEVELOPING THE ACTIVIST STYLE

▼ Split your study time up; never allow yourself to spend more than 30 minutes on one task. Make the task as diverse as possible, i.e. spend 30 minutes thinking about your lecture notes, then 30 minutes criticising a recent article that you have read.

▼ Put yourself in the limelight as often as possible. Volunteer to give a presentation or lead a seminar, or, alternatively, force yourself to contribute to group discussion. Remember, everyone is entitled to his/her own opinion, and yours is just as valid as anyone else's.

▼ Try bouncing your ideas off your peers. Hearing other people's points of view and having to defend yours will help you formulate new ideas and arguments. To start with, this will be easier in small groups. You could try setting up a study group with friends (see Section 2 for further information). As your confidence and abilities grow, you may find you are able to contribute more easily to large group discussions.

SUGGESTED TECHNIQUES FOR DEVELOPING THE REFLECTOR STYLE

▼ Carefully consider all sides of the argument and weigh up the evidence for and against each one before you contribute to a discussion or before you start writing an essay.

Successful Study

▼ Force yourself to practise not contributing in group discussions. Instead, listen carefully to what other people say and see how logically one comment follows on from another. Observe people's non-verbal behaviour: How do they signal that they want to speak? How do other people make it clear that they disagree?

▼ Set time aside to review your learning. Think about your strengths and weaknesses and formulate action plans to help you develop.

▼ Spend time producing a well-thought out and planned piece of written work. Do a draft first, and then keep reviewing and refining it until it is as good as it can be. Get friends to comment on your work. Ask them to look at spelling and grammar as well as content (see Section 3 for further information).

SUGGESTED TECHNIQUES FOR DEVELOPING THE THEORIST STYLE

▼ Write down the main theories in your subject area. Assimilate all the arguments and evidence for and against each theory. Think about how the theories are similar/dissimilar to each other. Try and establish what the underlying assumptions are.

▼ Read two conflicting articles. Analyse the main arguments and try and spot inconsistencies, illogical statements and weak evidence. Try and understand how the two authors have reached such different viewpoints on the same subject.

▼ Try setting goals for your work. Think about what you are aiming to achieve in each presentation, essay or piece of writing and then decide on the steps that you will need to take in order to achieve this.

1. Looking at Learning

SUGGESTED TECHNIQUES FOR DEVELOPING THE PRAGMATIST STYLE

▼ Try to apply the theory you have learnt to practical situations. Constantly ask yourself 'Is this true for me?'; 'What would happen if x variable was changed?'

▼ Learn about and practise different practical techniques. These could be techniques within your subject area, i.e. statistical analyses, or they could be techniques such as presentation, communication, writing, listening, etc. Learn from the ways that other people do things. Get others to scrutinise your techniques and ask for advice on how to improve.

▼ Immerse yourself in practical activities at every opportunity (i.e. carrying out project work, collecting data, gaining work experience, or interviewing people).

▼ Set yourself goals and devise action plans to meet these. Keep reviewing your progress against the goals and reformulate them if necessary.[2]

2. COGNITIVE PROCESSING OF MATERIAL

Writers[3] suggest that it is possible to learn at several different levels. This may depend on your study skills and/or the purpose of your learning.

The levels of learning are hierarchically arranged according to the level of cognitive processing that they require. They are as follows:

---

2. P. Honey and A. Mumford, *Using your Learning Styles* (Maidenhead: Pete Honey Publications, 1986).
3. B.S. Bloom, *Taxonomy of Educational Objectives: The Classification of Educational Goals*, Handbook 1 (New York: David Mackay, 1956).

Successful Study

1. Memorising facts.
2. Grasping the meaning of material.
3. Applying learned material to new situations. This could be applying rules, principles and methods.
4. Breaking down learned material into its component parts in order to understand the structure.
5. Putting the component parts of the learned material together to form a new structure, i.e. a new model/argument, etc.
6. Judging the value of the learned material, i.e. weighing up the evidence for and against.

Levels 1 and 2 are sometimes referred to as 'surface' levels of learning. Levels 3–6 are sometimes referred to as 'deep'[4] levels of learning. In some situations, it may be preferable to learn at the 'surface' level, i.e. learning facts for a multi-choice test. In other situations you may need to learn at the 'deep' level, i.e. presenting your own point of view in an essay, carrying out a research project. Some of you may already be learning at all levels in the hierarchy. Others may need a little help and guidance in order to begin to learn at the 'deep' level.

HOW DO YOU COGNITIVELY PROCESS MATERIAL?

Your reactions to the following statements will help you determine whether you usually learn at a 'deep' or at a 'surface' level.
Make a note of the statements which best describe you.[5]

---

4. F. Marton and R. Saljo, 'On Qualitative Differences in Learning', *British Journal of Educational Psychology*, Vol. 46 (1976), pp. 4-11.
5. N. Entwistle, *Styles of Teaching and Learning* (Chichester: Wiley, 1981).

1. Looking at Learning

(B) ✓ **1** I like to be told exactly what to do for essays, projects and assignments.

(B) **2** As I read I memorise important facts which I may want to use later on.

(B) ✓ **3** I am more interested in getting a good degree than I am in the courses that I am taking.

(A) ✓ **4** I always try and understand the meaning of what I am asked to read.

(A) ✓ **5** I often find myself questioning things that I hear in lectures or read in books.

(B) - **6** I try to memorise what we have done during the year for the exams.

(A) **7** I often follow up interesting topics or ideas that I have heard in lectures.

(A) ✓ **8** My main reason for being here is to learn more about subjects that really interest me.

(B) ✓ **9** I read quite a lot but I rarely seem to have time to really understand what I read.

(A) **10** I find the topics I am studying very interesting, and I will probably keep them up even after the course has finished.

(B) **11** I only read the books/articles which I need to read in order to do my assignments.

(A) **12** Even if something seems difficult, I keep trying until I understand it.

If you have ticked mostly (A)s then you are probably already able to learn at the 'deep' level. If you have ticked mostly (B)s, you may find that your current study skills are not appropriate for learning at the 'deep' level.

When reading, writing and listening to others most importantly you must:

Successful Study

- Think about the information you are gathering.
- Aim to understand its meaning.
- Weigh up the evidence (i.e. from your personal experience and from what you have heard/read in the past) and decide how true it is for you.

The remaining sections in this book are designed to help you address some of these areas.

Section 2 gives more information on:

- How to read for understanding.
- How to take relevant notes.
- How to improve your learning through collaboration with friends.

Section 3 gives more information on:

- How to develop your understanding and form your own opinions through writing essays, experimental reports and project journals.

2 SUCCESSFUL STUDY

THERE is little doubt that good study skills contribute to academic success. Many students, however, are rarely given advice or instructions on how to study. Tutors and lecturers seldom provide a rationale for studying, leaving it entirely up to the students. That is why many students do not know what is expected of them when they begin their course.

The transition from being a school pupil to being a student involves taking responsibility for your own learning. As a student, you are now responsible for what, when and how you study. You will find there is little supervision and feedback from your tutors, so in order to do well you must learn how to manage your time in the most effective way. Being a student involves taking responsibility for how you organise yourself and learning how to study more independently, both in the way you carry out your learning tasks and in your attitude to your subject.

CONTENTS

This section provides guidelines and study techniques which will help you learn more effectively and improve your study skills and confidence. It will enable you to become more aware of different learning approaches and will help you to get the best out of your course. It is in no way prescriptive. It is clear there is no universal way of learning, no 'one' correct way to study. Different students will use different strategies on different tasks, and it is up to you to find the ones which suit your individual learning style and learning situations.

HOW TO USE 'SUCCESSFUL STUDY'

This section shows you a number of strategies that you can adopt and choose from. Simply reading it will give you a more positive approach to ways of studying. Practise the techniques recommended. **Remember:** good organisation, motivation and efficient use of time and resources are also important. Clarify in your mind what you expect to get out of the course. Study the course curriculum and make sure you have a clear idea of what is involved in each course element.

You only get out what you put in.

TIME MANAGEMENT AND SELF-ORGANISATION

It is obvious that you cannot study all the time — your free time is important too. By organising your time more effectively, you will be able to have useful study periods **and** the time to enjoy yourself.

▼ A good tip to remember is that it is easier and wiser to work for, say, five hours a day all year than to try to cram everything in just before your exams. Students who do the latter inevitably do not do themselves justice and cause themselves undue stress.

PERSONAL TIME MANAGEMENT is a skill — it involves identifying areas of high and low priority and allocating your study time accordingly. It is important to recognise your own temperament and needs when planning your work. Do you work better in the day or at night, early or late? Self-awareness will help you set realistic targets, plan effective periods of leisure and undertake work at times when you are likely to achieve most.

If you are going to be effective in managing your time then you must set yourself realistic goals for your study and remind yourself

2. Successful Study

during the year of what they are and what you need to do to achieve them. It may help to set yourself daily, weekly or even termly schedules.

Good time management involves having the right attitude and good methodical practice.

In order to improve your time management you should:

- ▼ Draw up a fixed, weekly schedule identifying realistic and manageable goals for your work.
- ▼ Always start with the most important work.
- ▼ Begin at a time that suits you, but make it a regular time.
- ▼ Try to work on at least one major task a day.
- ▼ Prioritise work and put off all that is unimportant.
- ▼ Avoid interruptions! Take the phone off the hook; tell people you are busy and ask them to see you later on.
- ▼ Periodically review your goals and identify what you still have to do to meet them. If necessary, re-prioritise your work.

Make sure you reward yourself! Time management means making sure you have time to get the work done well and also to go out and have a good time.

As a student you have a high proportion of 'free' time, so use it constructively. **Remember:** learning is now **your** responsibility.

THE LIBRARY

Use its resources and your time here productively. Some of the important resources available in the library are:

- ▼ books (long- or short-term loan)
- ▼ periodicals
- ▼ bibliographies
- ▼ government publications

Successful Study

- inter-library loans
- dictionaries
- exam papers
- atlases
- audio-visual equipment
- CD-ROM
- photographic, photocopying, fax and telex services

> *There are ~~two classification~~ systems commonly used for books in the library:*

(i) **Computerised Cataloguing System:** the most efficient way to access books. It has an author and a subject index, so you can browse through either of these to find books.

(ii) **The Dewey Decimal System:** a system which allocates three-figure main numbers to each main branch of knowledge: 000 belongs to the 'generalities', 100 belongs to 'Philosophy and Related Disciplines', 200 belongs to 'Religion', and so on. Within these general groupings, branches of knowledge each have a subgroup, i.e. the 800s belong to 'Literature', the 810s to 'American Literature in English', the 820s to 'English and Anglo-Saxon Literature', and so on. Within these groupings, subject areas are further refined so that a book on any given subject can be classified exactly within its general group.

- Familiarise yourself with the Dewey numbers attached to your subject. It will help you get to the right area of the library.

Other sources of information

Dictionaries, encyclopaedias, directories, handbooks and manuals (provide concise information on one subject), journals, magazines

2. Successful Study

There is a wide range of sources of information

and newspapers — look at the periodicals taken regularly by your library. Current issues are usually on display, perhaps in a separate room.

Periodicals contain original and review articles in your subject area. These may be of interest and use to you. There are abstracting and indexing journals which help people undertaking a literature search to find articles that are likely to be of use. There are also computer-based information retrieval services. Once you have complete bibliographic details, a publication can be obtained on inter-library loan if it is not available in your own library.

You may also need collections of photographs, maps, recordings, tape-slide sets, videotapes and films. These may be available in an audio-visual aids section of the library, or they may be kept in map rooms or language laboratories, or other specialist rooms in appropriate teaching departments.

Do not forget that tutors, subject specialists and other professionals are also important sources of information.

When to use the library

The library is extremely important when you are working on an assessed thesis, dissertation or report and you need references. Also, when you are taking the final exams of, for example, a professional body, where you are required to be conversant with the latest developments in the field, access to a selection of specialist books and periodicals is essential.

The library also provides a **STUDY ATMOSPHERE.** There is space and quiet for study and many people find it helps their concentration. If you have time between lectures, it is quicker to go and work in the library than to go home.

TEACHING AND LEARNING METHODS

LEARNING FROM LECTURES

Lectures are the standard teaching mode in Higher Education. They tend to be a one-way communication process, where the lecturer gives you information and ideas about a subject and you write them down. Lectures usually last just under an hour.

It is common for students to write down everything they hear. This is not necessary! Getting the most out of lectures is all about understanding what is being said rather than merely reproducing in note form what you are being told.

The purpose of the lecture is to communicate a body of information to enable you to learn important concepts and principles, and to motivate you so that you appreciate the importance of the subject material.

2. Successful Study

Some strategies to help you

➤ *Note taking in lectures*

Write down key words, phrases, sentences — no preamble, asides or lecture orientation. Use **abbreviations** where possible, such as: **NB** (note particularly); **cf.** (compare); **ct.** (contrast); **e.g.** (for example); **p.** (page); **C19** (19th century); etc. Use **symbols**, i.e. **mm** (millimetres); **%** (per cent); = (equal to); ≠ (different from); < (less than); > (greater than); etc.

As you become more experienced, you could also use diagrams, 'mind maps', or flow charts. You could also include dates, quotations, new words, or definitions. You could use **sequential** notes or **creative pattern** notes (see page 32).

Remember: it is more important to **LISTEN** to and **UNDERSTAND** what you are being told rather than slavishly writing everything down. Listen actively, question, jot down queries, etc. Notes are your own personal record — there are no rules as to what they should look like. Be **selective** and make sure your notes

Try to understand lectures, not reproduce them

Examples of note formats[1]

Sequential notes

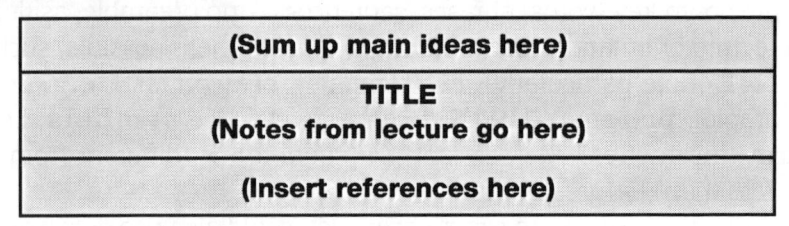

(Sum up main ideas here)
TITLE (Notes from lecture go here)
(Insert references here)

or ***Creative pattern notes***

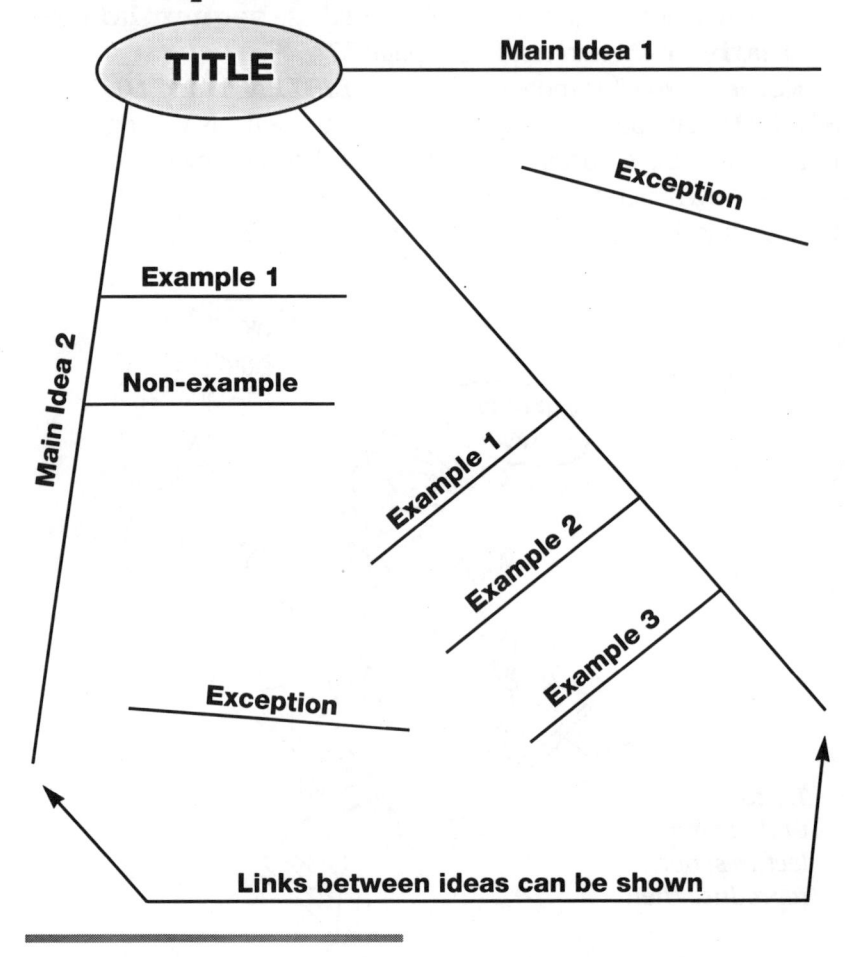

TITLE — Main Idea 1

Exception

Main Idea 2
- Example 1
- Non-example
- Example 1
- Example 2
- Example 3
- Exception

Links between ideas can be shown

---

1. K. Williams, *Study Skills* (London: Macmillan Education, 1989).

are legible! Some lectures will be more enjoyable than others — but you can still learn from the ones you don't enjoy.

- ▼ You should devise a note format which suits your needs. Note formats which leave you room to add further information later are important. You could write on alternate lines, leave wide margins, or write on only one side of the paper.

After the lecture

Recall the lecture and review your notes. Approximately 60% of the lecture is likely to be forgotten within 24 hours unless reinforced in some way, so it is important to do a follow-up activity on the same day.

➤ Some things to do

- ▼ Follow up references on booklists and handouts (the essential texts will usually be marked or asterisked).
- ▼ Work as a pair. Get a friend to take notes during a lecture, while you listen. Then swap roles in the next lecture.
- ▼ Discuss the lecture afterwards with some friends.
- ▼ **Don't** copy out your notes again — this is a waste of time. Instead, be selective when taking notes during the lecture.

Self-help groups

Self-help groups are simply informal groups of students who meet without a tutor to help each other with their learning. Giving help to each other is very useful: there is no better way of learning something than trying to teach it to someone else! Here are some guidelines for setting up a self-help group:

(a) Set the group up yourself! Don't wait for someone else to do it!

Successful Study

(b) Make sure everyone exchanges telephone numbers and addresses.

(c) Choose a chairperson who will take responsibility for arranging meetings.

(d) Regular meetings (e.g. every Wednesday at 11 am in the Students' Union Bar) are easier to remember and will get better attendance than meetings at irregular times and places.

(e) Try to plan ahead. If you can agree on a topic beforehand, people will know what to expect and will be able to prepare for the meeting.

(f) Allow time for general chat, even if this is not anything to do with the course. Although your time may be precious, the purpose of self-help groups is partly social. If you get too efficient, you may stop enjoying the meetings.

(g) Self-help groups don't have to be large: two people can meet together very productively.

(h) Self-help groups are particularly useful for revision if you have exams at the end of your course. Divide the course topics into sections and share these out between you. Each member of the group can revise one of the sections, present an overview to the group and then answer any questions.

(i) During the meetings you can: sort out queries about the course; exchange ideas and books before writing essays; read one another's essays; compare lecture notes; and work on group study activities, e.g. projects or presentations.

➤ **Belonging to a self-help group can**

▼ Increase your confidence and autonomy.

▼ Build up collaborative relationships.

2. Successful Study

▼ Improve your learning skills.

▼ Most importantly, make learning fun!

LEARNING FROM TUTORIALS AND SEMINARS

Tutorials and seminars involve small groups of students who meet every week with their tutor to discuss in more detail issues raised in the course. Tutorials and seminars are often much more effective than lectures, as they are designed to deepen your understanding of things, e.g. a theory, a text, or a case study. They develop your ability to listen, evaluate, argue, criticise and discuss.

It is **VERY IMPORTANT** to turn up to your tutorials as they provide a tight structure to your learning and you receive feedback and comments from essays, etc. It is wise to be **PREPARED** — read the text or material, form questions and ideas to talk about. You will sometimes have to give a seminar 'paper' where you present your own ideas on, or summary of, a subject.

In practice, tutorials frequently degenerate into knowledge-giving monologues by the tutor rather than interactive exchanges of information and ideas. **DON'T LET THIS HAPPEN!** Make sure you contribute! You may be shy or lack confidence, thinking that you are the only person that doesn't know anything or doesn't understand, but you are not. In most tutorials where no one speaks, people, including the tutor, are dying for someone to say something or ask a question. Don't waste a valuable learning opportunity!

It is up to you to get the discussion going. Don't let the tutor talk for you. Tutorials are your chance to speak up about your interests in the subject and give your opinions. Tutorials can be good for developing your confidence and interpersonal skills, as well as your understanding of a subject.

Successful Study

Don't let your tutorials become mini-lectures

Some strategies to help you

➤ Behaviour in tutorials and seminars

Adopt a looser strategy when taking notes than for lectures. Note down only the main points of a discussion, key ideas, etc. It is more important to listen and contribute rather than sit back passively and write everything down. The other students in the tutorial will have the same questions, difficulties and lack of knowledge, so you will help everyone if you raise questions yourself. Think about your level of involvement in the tutorial. Adopt any role you wish, e.g. devil's advocate, provocateur.

➤ Things to do to make the most of tutorials/seminars

Arrange times to meet with the other students outside appointed tutorial times. You can get a lot from group study and informal discussion, exchanging your ideas, etc. It also helps to consolidate the group, making people feel more comfortable about talking in tutorials.

2. Successful Study

It is important to keep up with the work set. If you have not done the reading, you won't have anything useful to contribute to the discussion. Some tutors allow time at the beginning of tutorials for students to prepare. If people are not covering the set work before class, suggest this to your tutor.

➤ Lectures and Tutorials

It is not the purpose of lectures and tutorials to indoctrinate. You should try to assimilate ideas that **you** are interested in and follow these up with independent study. **Remember:** there are many different interpretations of a subject area. Your tutor is not God. He or she welcomes challenging questions and candid thoughts on a subject. Use tutors as foundations and tools to guide your own learning.

Your tutor is not God!

OTHER TEACHING AND LEARNING METHODS

Practicals

Most practical work occurs in laboratories. However, fieldwork, placements and sandwich courses are also important methods for developing practical skills used in courses. The major goals of practical work are:

- ▼ Teaching manual and observational skills relevant to the subject.
- ▼ Improving understanding of methods of scientific enquiry.
- ▼ Developing problem-solving skills.
- ▼ Nurturing professional attitudes.

Most science and engineering students spend between 50% and 70% of their contact time in laboratory work. In laboratories, organised opportunities can be provided for you to appreciate and practise a range of skills and techniques relevant to your subject.

Whenever you have the opportunity to do practical work, ensure that you carry out the following:

- ▼ Obtain as much information as you can on the materials and equipment you will be using, i.e. the properties of the metal, wood or plastic and the procedures, apparatus, etc. involved.
- ▼ Develop your ability to:
    - (i) use the equipment
    - (ii) make observations
    - (iii) record your observations
    - (iv) develop your own procedures to solve problems.
- ▼ Learn to analyse what you or someone else is doing.

2. Successful Study

Remember: it is important to clarify to yourself what the emphasis is on in the practical and what the process of scientific enquiry means in your discipline.

Project work

Project work forms an important part of many courses and takes a variety of different forms: short or long; group or individual. Projects are an enjoyable and valuable way to learn. Projects enable you to explore a field that interests you in some depth and to develop your initiative, resourcefulness, research techniques and problem-solving skills. Importantly, projects require you to take responsibility for your own learning.

Depending on your subject, your project may involve you in desk research, in experimental laboratory work, in the production of a dramatic play, in the use of social research techniques, or in the production of an artefact such as a computer programme or a chair or a plan for a house. You will usually have to produce a project report, explaining what you did, why and how you did it and what the outcome was.

It is important to choose a project you are interested in. Projects will take up much of your time so it is important that you do something that you like. You are the key project resource.

Find out what is expected in your project from your project supervisor. Read project reports from previous years. Do you have to do a presentation at the end? Halfway through? Is there a length restriction? Is there a specific format to follow? What other resources are available to you?

Be aware of your time commitment to the project. There will inevitably be constraints and it is important to maintain the balance between the time spent on the project and on work from other courses. Put together a plan with information on when reports or presentations are due, your workload and other factors that will influence your work. Discuss this with friends or with your supervisor. **Remember:** organisation and communication are key factors which will influence the success of the project.

Group projects

Project work on many courses is undertaken by groups rather than individuals. You must work on your project, produce ideas and final reports/presentations together. Section 4, 'Grappling with Group Work', gives detailed information on how to carry out a group project.

Even if you are doing an individual project it is useful to discuss your approach with others — it can often lead to new ideas and help put your work into perspective.

➤ It is also useful to

- ▼ Keep a project diary in which you note down the things you do as you go along.

- ▼ Keep full notes of any data you collect and a bibliography.

- ▼ Consult previous project reports available in the library — these are extremely valuable to get a feel for what is required.

READING

In every sense of the word, you have to 'read' for your degree, whether it is a pure maths text, a poem, a seventeenth-century diary, a legal document or a biochemical journal. Reading lists can be daunting, but do not panic.

You are not expected to read everything on the list. 'Essential' items will usually be marked in some way, or ask your tutor or lecturer if you're unsure which texts are most important to read. It is useful to try to get some idea of the relative importance and the general subject matter of each text.

Your courses will require a whole range of different kinds of reading for different purposes. You will find that you will adopt different strategies to suit your needs. Before you begin, define your reading goals. Ask yourself: 'Why am I reading this text?'; 'How is

2. Successful Study

it relevant?'; 'What am I getting from it that is new to me?' Think about how and why each text fits into the course.

Some strategies to help you

Here is a simple method of planning your reading so that it is more active, more purposeful, and much more productive.

SQ3R stands for:[2]
Survey   Question   Read   Recall   Review

➤ *Survey*
Have a quick look through the book (or chapter, or article) to see what it is about and what you can expect to get out of it. You may also find it helpful to survey the list of contents and the index.

➤ *Question*
Write down the questions you will be able to answer when you have read the book (or chapter, or article) properly. The survey you have just done and your own needs (and maybe assignment titles and exam questions) will help you to formulate the questions.

➤ *Read*
Once you have got some useful questions, reading is easy. All you have to do is find where the answers to your questions are and read those bits carefully, perhaps making a few notes, sketching one or two diagrams, doing some calculations, and so on. As soon as you have answered all your questions, get out of the book as soon as you can. Books have a habit of sucking in the unwary and wasting their time. Don't read any more than you absolutely have to! Summaries at the end of a chapter can be very useful in helping you to use your reading time effectively.

---

2. K. Williams, *Study Skills* (London: Macmillan, 1989).

Successful Study

➤ Recall

Try to answer all your questions without looking at the book or your notes. You will soon find out what you have learned and what you need to spend more time on.

➤ Review

Go back to the book to check that your answers are right. Go over the things you have got wrong or could not answer. Do not get trapped by the book again! Just dip into the relevant bits.

Reading flexibly

In reality, effective reading is about being flexible and purposeful, not about how fast you can read. The faster people read, the less they get out of reading. However, here are some effective reading techniques which will improve and develop your reading skills and aid your learning.

Reading as an active process

These are basic reading skills well worth practising.

Scanning — for when you want to find a particular item of information. Scan the contents pages or index so that you can go to the relevant pages. Look for particular words and read carefully.

Skimming — for when you want to gain a quick impression of a text or article. You do not need to read every word — note signposts: chapter headings, sub-headings, bold print, italics, lists, etc. Read the first sentence of each paragraph. Read for an overview.

Deep Study Reading — for reading actively to make connections, understand meanings, consider implications and evaluate arguments. Reading deeply involves a six-point strategy:

2. Successful Study

▼ Understand the purpose of the reading task.

▼ Recall relevant prior knowledge of the subject.

▼ Identify important content and focus on it. Don't give equal concentration to content of less or trivial importance.

▼ Make a conscious attempt to evaluate the content for internal consistency, compatibility with prior knowledge and with common sense.

▼ Monitor your own reading. Review your understanding of the text periodically.

▼ Make and test inferences deliberately, including interpretations, predictions and conclusions.

Note taking during reading

Adopt an analytical approach. **Remember:** always read critically. Don't laboriously copy out reams of the text. Note down what you want to remember. Remember your reading aims and goals; they will sharpen your reading. Make brief, concise notes. Record key words, phrases and sentences. Add your own comments and evaluation. Write **SUMMARIES** of what you have read. **Remember:** one author's interpretation may differ from another's, so weigh the evidence presented. Make up your own mind.

NB: Be careful always to write down sources of information, i.e. the page number, title, author, date of publication, publisher, etc.

WRITING

Writing assigned tasks causes much anxiety! Writing is a painful process, so many students put it off, saying **'I will just read a little more'**, or **'I will start tomorrow'**. It is usually preferable to write at one sitting once you have gathered all your information and facts together. **Remember:** always keep in mind the essay question and what you are writing. Articulate your goals: Who is this for? Do I need to say this? Would this be better at the beginning or end? Remember to plan your essay.

If you find the writing process difficult and are unsure how to set about writing an essay, get hold of other essays students have written and study the way they have written them. Ask your tutor, who will suggest specific stylistic points, diagnose problems or suggest alternative ways of structuring and organising the material. Section 3, 'Wrestling with Writing', contains more information and advice.

NB: Make as much use of the library as you can. Read good prose regularly. This is necessary even for scientists and engineers, not only arts students. There is a lot of donkey-work involved in writing essays, but it is a very effective way of making the subject matter your own.

ASSESSMENT

Examinations and assessed work play an important part in the course of your life as a student. What you do in exams and assessed work counts.

Not everyone will have an exam at the end of his/her course — your course may be continuously assessed in the form of written essays, objective tests, reports, case studies, projects, orals, etc. Find out about the assessment procedures and course objectives for your course before you start. Be clear in your own mind what you have to achieve in order to pass your course. It is important to familiarise yourself with the pattern of assessment and the types of examination questions you are likely to get. They provide you with an indication of the relative importance the department gives to the course objectives.

2. Successful Study

Assessment

Assessment patterns vary enormously from course to course and they are most important in how you plan your work for the year. The variables to look for are:

- ▼ What sort of assessment tasks will you be asked to do, i.e. project work, essays, problem sheets, short note answers or multiple choice questions?

- ▼ How are the assessment tasks spaced out over the year? Is there a pattern of continuous assessment or does all the assessment happen in end-of-year, or even end-of-course, examinations? How long are you allowed for each piece of assessed course work? How long are the exams and how many questions do you have to complete?

- ▼ What is the relative importance of each piece of assessed work? What marks does it carry? How does it contribute to your overall assessment?

- ▼ What are the consequences of failure in any one assessment task? Can you resit exams/resubmit assessed work? In some cases you may have to repeat a year or even leave the course if you fail on certain tasks.

- ▼ How predictable are the assessment tasks? Are they more or less the same from year to year? Do you get to see your exam questions in advance or not?

GROUP ASSESSMENT and **SELF-ASSESSMENT** may also play a part in your course. You may be asked as a group to allocate marks to your peers on the basis of what you think they have achieved and how well they have gone about it. It is useful to agree criteria for peer assessment before you begin the group task, for example: attendance at meetings, contribution of ideas, research work, etc.

Self-assessment involves you establishing the criteria and standards you will apply to your work and then making judgements about the degree to which you have met them.

Successful Study

Peer and self assessment may seem very threatening. However, developing a sense of judgement of yourself and of others is an important skill to learn. Peer assessment is the way that most professional organisations, e.g. doctors, lawyers, engineers, etc., operate, either to give rewards or practise discipline.

The key to successful group and peer assessment is to agree the criteria in advance and to be honest and constructive.

NB: The hidden curriculum

The stated aims and contents of the course are the visible curriculum. However, there are quite often mismatches between the stated aims of a course and what you actually have to do to pass it. For example, the stated aims of the course may include developing communication and independent research skills, yet the course may only be assessed by unseen examinations. It pays to examine your course carefully to see if you can discover any hidden curriculum. Discuss this with your tutors.

Some strategies to help you

➤ Preparing for exams

First, consider what is expected of you. Then collect the relevant information — get together a statement about course objectives, the syllabus, your lecture and tutorial notes, your own notes from texts, past exam papers, comments on essays you have written, critical works, etc. Next, select your material. Be 'cue-conscious' — look to the staff for hints about possible exam questions. Let your tutor help you. Don't fall into the misbelief that the exam system is impenetrable and marking is infallible.

NB: REVISION PREPARATION means long-term preparation, keeping up with the work as you go along and revising regularly. When you come to revising you should not be learning subjects from scratch.

2. Successful Study

➤ *Revision techniques*

Plan a revision timetable. Make it sensible, realistic and stick to it! Start revising six to eight weeks before your first exam. Revise your weakest topics first. Give each topic sufficient time, reflecting its importance and difficulty. Use past papers (two years is enough) and plan answers to them. Make short concise notes, aiming to outline main themes and issues that you have identified from lectures and your reading. You could record these on index or swot cards, or you could use mind-mapping or creative note-taking techniques. Discuss topics with friends and tutors. Do not get bogged down by small detail. Understanding is the key! You should be formulating arguments and opinions backed up by facts.

Get together with some friends or with a study group and revise together helping each other out with problems and filling in gaps for each other. Either in a group or individually:

- ▼ Set yourself questions.
- ▼ Solve problems.
- ▼ Organise your knowledge.
- ▼ Make notes of gaps.
- ▼ Prepare topic outlines.
- ▼ Recall main points.
- ▼ Use different sources of information — try to get the latest revision of each book you consult.
- ▼ Concentrate on essentials.

Have frequent breaks — every 20–30 minutes or so. Chat to a friend, make a coffee. Revise where it suits you best — the library, a quiet study room at University or College, or at home.

NB: The object of revision is not to rehearse answers but to remind yourself of facts and theories and to use them flexibly. Do not make unreasonable demands on yourself — no one can know everything about a subject — choose areas that interest you and apply yourself to them.

Successful Study

Don't panic!

> **Summary of things to do when revising**
>
> ▼ See a good selection of exam papers.
>
> ▼ Keep to a sensible revision plan covering all the topics.
>
> ▼ Give yourself a mock exam.
>
> ▼ Ask tutors for help, or counsellors if you are over-anxious.
>
> ▼ Do not miss organised revision classes.

> **Exam technique**

Do not panic! If you have revised thoroughly you should do yourself justice. Be positive — exams are a challenge and an opportunity to display your knowledge and understanding.

2. Successful Study

- Read the paper carefully to make sure you understand what you are required to do.
- Select questions as directed on the paper.
- Consider what is required in each answer before writing.
- Allocate your time according to the marks available.
- Look at the verb in the question. Do what it says.
- Plan your answers.
- Clarify your understanding of the question — use words from the question or appropriate points in your answer.
- Do not attempt questions you do not understand.
- Do easy ones first.
- Answer the question precisely. Do not include irrelevant material or repeat yourself. Keep to your usual style — there is no time to worry about the structure of your sentences.
- Remember that the first marks in every question are the easiest to get.
- Answer the required number of questions.
- Check and edit your answers.

In summary, there is no 'one' correct way to study. There are many techniques that work for some people and not for others. The secret of successful study is to develop your own approach drawing on techniques that work for you.

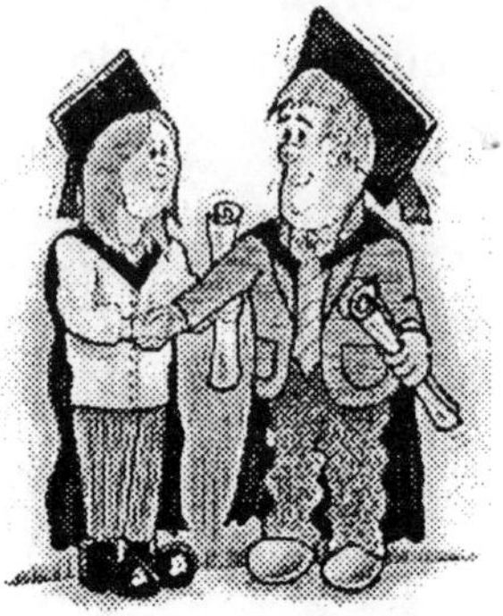

3 WRESTLING WITH WRITING

WRITTEN communication is an essential part of modern life. For students the ability to write well is particularly important.

The following guidelines aim to help make written work less stressful and more successful.

Different academic disciplines demand different types of written work and each person has an individual writing style. These guidelines should not be taken as a set of rules. They should be used as an aid to improving your confidence and ability when performing written tasks.

CONTENTS

This section outlines the stages you should go through in producing a piece of written work. Details of some of the necessary techniques, e.g. managing your time and effective reading, are presented in Section 2, 'Successful Study'.

HOW TO USE 'WRESTLING WITH WRITING'

You should read this section before you begin a writing task. As with any other skill, you may have to practise some of the techniques described until they become second nature. The 'Rewriting and Proofing' section provides a useful checklist for all writing tasks.

FINDING OUT WHAT IS EXPECTED

It is important to be as clear as possible about what your task is. Before starting to write, you should try to establish exactly what is expected of you.

There are many different types of writing.

An **essay** is an informal prose composition in which the writer displays knowledge and opinions. There is a variety of types of essay questions: 'Compare and contrast . . .' and 'Discuss the relative advantages of . . .' are fairly common. Similarly, there is a variety of possible essay structures. Generally, essays should contain some form of introduction where you outline the background and aims for your essay, a large 'body' where you argue your case, and a conclusion where you summarise your arguments.

The structure of **reports** is less variable. A report is a document in which the writer presents specific information as concisely and accurately as possible. A good report is characterised by its objectivity and systematic presentation. Planning is essential.

A report should have an **introduction** where the terms of reference or topic are defined. Essential background material may also be included.

The introduction should be followed by any or all of the following:

    Method   where you tell your reader how you went about getting or analysing the information for the report.

3. Wrestling with Writing

Results where you present your findings.

Discussion where you discuss the implications of your findings.

Summary where you summarise your results and make recommendations on the basis of your findings.

Besides essays and reports, there is a wide variety of other types of writing. These can range from a legal opinion to a book review, from an experimental report to a project journal.

If you are uncertain about the right format for a piece of writing, **ask** your lecturer, tutor or supervisor to explain. They may have an example which they can show you. Knowing the correct format and style is very important. It affects the way you think about the entire project, from how you research it to how you set out each page.

UNDERSTANDING THE QUESTION

If the subject or topic for your piece of written work is set by a tutor or lecturer, rather than set by yourself, ensure that you understand the question before you try to answer it. If you are uncertain about what it means, ask your friends, a lecturer or supervisor. It is vital that you have a correct understanding of what you are expected to write about. Even the best researched and written essay will not get a good result if it is answering the wrong question.

While you are writing it is helpful periodically to refer back to your question or subject topic to ensure that you are still on track. Doing this also helps to refocus your ideas and may sometimes lead you to think of new approaches. Sometimes discussing the topic with friends and classmates can help you to understand it and gain fresh insights for your answer.

If your topic is a broad one, or you have the opportunity to set your own topic, make sure that what you plan to do has clearly

Successful Study

defined boundaries and is suitable. You can do this by asking your tutors for information or by getting them to prepare guidance materials and examples for you.

Make sure that you have a **clear** understanding of your topic, subject or problem before you start to write. **Relevance is a key concept in good writing.**

TIME ALLOCATION

It is important to allocate your time effectively when writing. Try to estimate how much time you will need for researching as well as writing. The more writing you do the better you will get at estimating how long each project will take. Initially, it is safer to overestimate the time you think it will take to complete a piece of work.

While some people feel they work best under pressure, leaving work until the last minute should be avoided. Not only because rushed work is often recognised and marked accordingly, but also because poor planning can become a habit. This habit will not only ensure that your writing has no chance to improve, but it also makes for a lot of stress.

3. Wrestling with Writing

When preparing to write, remember time will be needed for:
1. Finding source material
2. Reading
3. Planning
4. Writing
5. Rewriting and proofing

Each one of these steps is equally important.

1. Finding source material

Learn to use your library. Think about the question and jot down ideas that you may wish to find more information about. Ask your librarian to help you if you have difficulty finding what you are looking for. Knowing how to use the various reference tools in the library will not only allow you to find material quickly, it may also guide you to some less obvious sources. If these extra sources are relevant, they can improve your work considerably.

A PRACTICAL NOTE: Finding the books and articles you need is not as easy as simply knowing the right place to look. Large numbers of students are looking for small numbers of books. Finding source material can be a time-consuming and frustrating task. Try working as a group and sharing resources if you all have the same question.

Successful Study

While it is important to find a comprehensive range of source material, try not to over-research. Finding material can be a much more pleasurable activity than actually having to write about it. Be careful not to fall into the trap of virtuously stacking up more and more material which you will never have time to read. **Be selective.**

2. Reading

Reading source material can be very time-consuming. Remember this when you are gathering your information and try to estimate how long it will take to read.

Take notes as you read. Remember, you don't have to read the whole book. Only some parts will be relevant. Scan contents pages, indexes, and headings to ensure that you read what you need to read. Note down page numbers and headings when taking notes as this will save considerable time and frustration when it comes to the time to pull all of your notes together. (Section 2 has more information on effective reading techniques.)

Reading can be very interesting and is an excellent delaying tactic. Ask yourself, as you approach each book, what you hope to get from it. Make sure you have a good reason for getting involved in a book and that you are not just doing it to put off starting your essay.

3. Planning

How you plan your writing depends largely on what your topic is.

A plan can be written down or just kept in your head. Whichever way you choose, it is important to remember that a plan must be flexible. It should act as a useful guide only.

The key to planning is organisation. Your material and ideas should be sorted into themes or sections. Often your topic may be split into different ideas and you can use each of these ideas as the theme to group your material around. Grouping your material also provides another opportunity to ensure that it is all relevant.

3. Wrestling with Writing

Once your materials are grouped, you should think about what order you want to present them in. Ordering your ideas is very important. If you have difficulty deciding what the best order is, discuss this with a classmate or friend. Do not get stuck at this stage. Remember this is only a plan, and you can always change it. Just try to find a logical sequence. Sometimes it can be helpful to write this sequence down using each theme as a subheading.

➤ Sample plan

Title ▼ *Article on Introduction of Student-Centred Learning into Practical Work*

Aims
- ▼ 1. Show how provision of extra learning experiences motivates and empowers students
- ▼ 2. Show that students take advantage of opportunities and that they get more out of course

Introduction
- ▼ Background to traditional teaching in practicals
- ▼ New approach
- ▼ Presentation of aims

Assessment
- ▼ Outline method and statistics
- ▼ Present evidence that better learning occurred
- ▼ TABLES of Time 1 and Time 2 results

Discussion
- ▼ Build on results, add anecdotal/qualitative evidence
- ▼ Discuss findings
- ▼ Implications/drawbacks
- ▼ Conclusion

Your plan can be written as a flow diagram or as a list. This will give you an outline for your writing task. When you write your plan, leave space under each subheading to insert ideas and notes of material to be included. Underline the points which you most wish to emphasise.

Once your plan is complete, check to ensure that you have added all of your relevant material. If you have some references which are not mentioned on the plan, check to see why.

Decide on what illustrative material (tables, graphs, photographs, quotations, etc.) you are going to use. Make sure this material is effective and make a note of where you want to use it on your plan. Remember to comment on and label any illustrations and tables you may include in your text.

Make your plan as brief or as detailed as you want. For some people a brief plan is the best, especially if you have a good memory and find getting your ideas onto paper easy. For others a detailed plan can mean that the actual task of writing becomes simplified, as it may only involve putting each subheading into sentence form and expanding on the ideas you have listed below it.

Whichever way you choose to do the plan, be aware of the time frame you are working to, and resist the temptation to use planning as a delaying tactic if you are someone who has difficulty starting to write.

Planning, in fact the whole process of writing, involves reflection and alteration. You may read a little, draw up a rough plan, read some more, change your plan, think, then change your plan again as you get a better understanding of your topic and a clearer idea of how you are going to present it. Going back to a plan and changing it and then back to your source material is common and can be very beneficial.

4. *Writing*

It is helpful if you think of your initial attempt as a draft only. The time it takes to write varies. Some people find that they write best using one long uninterrupted session. Others concentrate best over short periods of time and need lots of breaks. Whichever method

3. Wrestling with Writing

works best for you, ensure that you have plenty of time left to rewrite and to make additions later. Use your plan as a guide.

You may either write by hand or using a word processor. Increasingly, departments require student work to be word processed. The main advantage for staff is that this ensures essays and reports are legible. The advantages of using a word processor for your work are many. You can chop and change work without having to rewrite it, you can add notes and comments as you write, then delete them later on, and you develop basic IT skills which will be useful in later life. Disadvantages of using a computer for your work are that, unless you have one of your own, you can't write at home, and if you can't type, writing your report or essay may take some time. However, practice makes perfect!

If you are writing by hand, leave a wide margin and space between lines to allow for notes and corrections.

Use your plan to work from and be careful not to get bogged down by re-reading your source materials. These should already be well explored. What is important at this stage is getting your ideas down in sentence form on paper. They do not need to be perfectly expressed. Keep to the point and **keep going**. If you need to take breaks, make sure you return to your task as soon as you can. If you find yourself stuck on a particular point, make a quick note and continue.

5. Rewriting and Proofing

How many times you rewrite and how extensive your rewrite will depend on the success of your draft and how close you think you are to the finished product.

At the very least, your first draft should give you a comprehensive base to work with. In order to rewrite your draft effectively you should ask yourself the following questions. While considering these questions, compare what you have written with your plan and with the original question or subject topic.

(a) Is **everything** that you have written relevant to the topic?

Successful Study

(b) Has anything essential been left out?

(c) Have you adequately emphasised important points?

(d) Are your ideas ordered in a logical way?

(e) Is it the required length?

(f) Are all the illustrations and tables clearly explained and indexed?

(g) If you have used technical terms or symbols, are they sufficiently explained?

(h) Have you used appropriate vocabulary and level of writing?
 The complexity of the language you use will depend largely on what you are writing. Many disciplines have their own language (or jargon) which you may need to use.

3. Wrestling with Writing

The people who you expect to read your work will have a major effect on the style of your writing. It is clear that a lyrical, poetic style of writing would not be suitable for a scientific report. The materials you have found to base your writing on should give you an indication of what type of vocabulary and style to use. You can also find work from past students, or ask your supervisor or classmates to get an idea about appropriate vocabulary.

A good starting point is to remember that short and simple is best. Make sure that you have a clear understanding of the words, particularly jargon or technical phrases that you have used. If you are in any doubt, use a reference book or dictionary to check.

(i) Is your spelling correct?

Use your dictionary to check your spelling. Do this thoroughly. If you are using a word processor with a 'spellcheck' function do not rely only on this. You should still check the spelling yourself.

(j) Have you used punctuation correctly?

Appropriate punctuation will help to clarify your writing, as it affects not only interpretation but sentence structure.

(k) How well have you structured your sentences?

The sentence structure you use will be determined by the type of writing you are doing and your own personal style. Essays and scientific reports may be written impersonally (e.g. 'it was found . . .'; 'recommendations were made that . . .'), while book reviews or project journals are more likely to be written in a personal style (e.g. 'I thought that . . .'; 'my interpretation of . . .').

As a rule, short sentences are best as they convey ideas the most clearly. However, it is important to vary sentence length, otherwise your writing can become list-like or disjointed.

Successful Study

(l) How well are your paragraphs ordered?

Think carefully about the way you group your sentences into paragraphs. Each paragraph should have its own theme. If the theme changes mid-paragraph, this may be a signal that a new paragraph is needed.

If you have doubts about your paragraphing, look at the reference material you found the most helpful and compare its paragraph length and structure to your own.

(m) Have you correctly quoted and referenced your source materials?

This is very important for several reasons. First, it allows the reader to check the accuracy of your statements and to see what they were based on. Secondly, it gives readers somewhere to start from should they wish to do their own research. Thirdly, referencing highlights your own opinions by clearly defining which ideas come from other people.

Failure to reference can lead your readers to suspect that you are trying to pass someone else's ideas off as your own. This is an impression that must be avoided, as it is a form of theft known as plagiarism. Plagiarism will, **at the least**, have a bad effect on your final mark.

Different types of writing have different referencing systems, as do different subject areas. It is important that you ask your supervisor or classmates if you do not know how to reference. Working from an example is the best way to learn how to reference for your subject.

Plagiarism is theft

3. Wrestling with Writing

Having considered the thirteen questions above and satisfied yourself that you have done all you can do, your task is almost complete. At this stage it is a good idea to get a classmate or friend to read your work. Ask them to proof it as you have. It is particularly useful to have someone else's opinion regarding the clarity, legibility and structure of your writing. It is not too late to make changes at this stage, so discuss your writing and apply what you learn.

IMPORTANT POINTS TO REMEMBER

- ▼ Keep your writing logical, relevant and easy to understand.
- ▼ Remember that the reader must be able to understand the points you are trying to make from reading alone — there is no opportunity for the reader to ask questions.
- ▼ Writing effectively for different audiences is a skill which will improve with practice.
- ▼ Don't be scared by blank sheets of paper. Writing is simply a way of communicating your understanding of a subject to another person as you would in a conversation.
- ▼ Don't get bogged down in piles of books.
- ▼ Don't put things off until you are on the verge of a minor breakdown.
- ▼ Read selectively around the subject; plan carefully but flexibly, and the rest will follow.

4 GRAPPLING WITH GROUP WORK

BEING in a group is part of being a human, a social animal. This section aims to introduce you to

- ▼ The idea of working in groups.
- ▼ Some of the processes that go on in groups.
- ▼ Some knowledge of the factors that make a successful group.

It does not try to answer every question you may have about group work nor to make you an effective leader in five minutes. It will give you a few ideas about yourself and about groups to think about next time you find yourself working with other people.

Successful Study

It seems to be a common assumption that everyone knows how to work well in a group and how to get the most out of participating in a group. Unfortunately, this is not always the case.

Working in groups is an inevitable part of life, whether studying or otherwise, at work or at play. Formally, a group could be said to be two or more people who interact regularly to pursue some common goal. A sports team, a tutorial group, and a 'project team' are all formal groups. A group of friends at a pub is an informal group. Twenty people standing at a bus stop is not a group at all. The sort of group that this section aims to help you work in is the small group (less than eight members) assigned a specific task, such as solving a problem or doing a project.

CONTENTS

This section contains background notes about groups and their workings, a guide for completing a typical student group work activity, and a set of questions for you to consider when working in groups.

HOW TO USE 'GRAPPLING WITH GROUP WORK'

The guidance notes should be read before you start work in your group to give you some background to the process of group work. The questions can be used at any time during the group work, either individually or with other group members, to help you reflect on your development as a group member and on the development of the group as a whole. The questions are not meant to be a definitive list, but merely a starting point for your own reflection and discussion.

4. Grappling with Group Work

NOTES ON GROUPS

'If a camel is a horse designed by a group, why do groups exist?'

Formal groups exist, or are made, for a number of purposes. Often these purposes overlap. Groups can bring together a wide range of skills and talents that one single individual could not possess. This is particularly useful for complex problem solving, making difficult decisions and for collecting ideas. By involving a number of people in a group, one can also increase people's commitment to a solution or plan. If everybody has contributed or feels they 'own' the solution they are more likely to support and defend it.

GROUP BEHAVIOUR

Behaviour in groups is generally classified as falling into two categories: behaviour specifically related to doing the work (task-oriented behaviour), and behaviour related specifically to promoting the continued existence of the group (group maintenance behaviour). 'Task-oriented' behaviour includes deciding who does what, coming up with ideas, gathering, sharing and interpreting information, and developing, testing and implementing solutions. 'Group maintenance' behaviour, on the other hand, aims to improve relationships between group members, maintain group cohesion, and to manage and resolve conflict within the group.[1]

The importance of, and the proportion of time spent on, each type of behaviour will vary throughout the lifetime of the group. In the early stages of a group's existence, most time is usually spent, formally or informally, on 'group maintenance' behaviour. This is

---

1. K. Wexley and L. Yukl, *Organizational Behavior and Personnel Psychology* (Illinois: Richard D. Irwin, 1984).

DON'T NEGLECT GROUP MAINTENANCE BEHAVIOUR

not surprising as groups need to establish themselves, roles need to evolve, initial conflicts and problems need to be solved, and the levels of trust, openness and commitment within the group need to be found. Unfortunately for those who want to complete the task as soon as possible, this stage is almost inevitable. Once this initial phase has been completed, however, the group's emphasis shifts to 'task-oriented' activity, and 'group maintenance' takes a secondary position.

ROLES

A number of different roles exist within groups. The sort of roles you play will depend, in part, on your personality and on the nature of the group. In the sort of groups that you will be working in (small and democratic, i.e. no one assigns roles from outside), the roles that people play will evolve over time. Studies[2] have shown that the following roles are played in effective groups:

---

2. M. Belbin, *Management Teams: Why they Succeed or Fail* (London: Heinemann, 1981).

4. Grappling with Group Work

- A **leader**, who co-ordinates the team's efforts and ensures all opinions are heard and considered.
- A **shaper**, who pushes the group on to achieve the task.
- A **plant**, who is the main source of creative and original ideas.
- A **critic**, who dissects ideas and finds flaws in arguments.
- A **liaison person**, who brings new ideas and contributions from outside the group and helps prevent the group from becoming too inward-looking.
- A **practical person**, who turns ideas into manageable tasks.
- A **team worker**, who is supportive of other group members and helps hold the group together.
- A **finisher**, who checks details and ensures deadlines are met.

Successful Study

Obviously, one person can play more than one of these roles within the same group. It is important however, for the effective completion of the task and the continued existence of the group that all the roles are played. Too much of one role may result in an ineffective group. Different people with different approaches are important for a successful group.

▰▰▰ *SUCCESSFUL GROUPS*

Other characteristics of a successful and effective group are that group members feel confident about offering more than one point of view or contribution, no matter how tentative, and that group members are responsive to, and appreciative of, different points of view and contributions. Importance is given to seeking and listening to the views of each member. In other words, the atmosphere within the group is supportive and open, which makes people feel good because their opinions seem to be valued.

Working in a group, by its very nature, means that your actions will not just affect yourself but also your fellow group members. If you arrange a time to meet, you are letting the whole group down by not turning up. It is vital that arrangements for meetings are made clear to all group members so that everyone knows what is happening and can attend. You will quickly learn how annoying it is when people don't turn up for meetings.

4. Grappling with Group Work

It is also important to remember that working in a group will mean that you probably won't get your own way. Compromise is an inescapable part of group work. Remember though that the concessions you make will probably result in a better final solution than if you were doing it by yourself.

A GUIDE FOR COMPLETING A TYPICAL STUDENT GROUP WORK ACTIVITY

This guide is based on an imaginary group project, e.g. a design project or a research project. It is important that you realise that it is your responsibility to clarify and come to an agreement with staff members about the requirements for the group, i.e. the minimum number of meetings required, help available, contact with staff, etc., and the type of assessment for the group work before the project commences. While staff should have made this clear to you, it is up to you to make sure that they do.

As a first step the group should clarify for themselves exactly what it is they have been asked to do. Getting the question right is an important, and often neglected, part of getting the solution right.

Having pin-pointed what you are supposed to be doing, the next stage is to generate ideas about how best to do it. You may decide that information needs to be gathered or some other task needs to be carried out to better inform this stage. Tasks will have to be allocated to group members. People will generally be happy to do things they like doing, but unfortunately there is usually some task that no one wants to do. It is important that the unwanted tasks are shared evenly among group members. **It is vital that attention is paid to the project deadlines, and that time limits are set for these tasks.**

Successful Study

Tasks will then be completed by group members on their own, before coming back to the rest of the group and presenting their findings. The group must then assimilate this information. Based on this groundwork, the group may generate a solution or strategy to achieve the goal. This may take some time, coming up with ideas and then evaluating each one. It is often useful to dedicate a limited amount of time solely to generating ideas. In this time no idea should be criticised or commented on. After this time ideas should be questioned and discussed before one is decided upon.

Once this idea has been agreed, it must then be turned into action, broken into manageable tasks and allocated to group members. Individuals then carry out their tasks. After this, the group takes on a monitoring role, meeting to receive progress reports from individuals, to re-allocate tasks where necessary and to make sure things are going smoothly and to schedule.

Finally the group will draw together the results from individual tasks to produce the final report or presentation.

SOME HINTS

- ▼ **Listen to others.**
- ▼ **Value other people's contributions.**
- ▼ **Remember groups take a while to become 'comfortable'.**
- ▼ **Groups take time to get things done.**
- ▼ **Don't let your fellow group members down.**

4. Grappling with Group Work

LISTEN TO OTHERS

SOME REFLECTION

These questions may help you reflect on and learn from your experiences in groups.

- ▼ What are the advantages and disadvantages of groups?
- ▼ What is my role in the group?
- ▼ Why do I play this role?
- ▼ Has my role changed? How?
- ▼ How has the group changed?

Successful Study

- What stages has it gone through?
- How was/is conflict resolved?
- How comfortable does it feel to introduce new ideas to the group?
- What makes it feel like that?
- How does the group balance 'group maintenance' and 'task-oriented' behaviour?
- Do other group members' roles change in 'group maintenance' compared to 'task-oriented' behaviour?
- How successful was the group?
- How do I feel I have contributed to the success of the group?
- What more could I have done?
- What more could others have done?

5 SIMPLE SOLUTIONS

PROBLEM SOLVING is an activity which occurs not only in formal tasks given to individuals or groups, but also in situations encountered in everyday life. Problem solving involves individuals or groups in a process whereby they attempt to attain a solution to a problem that faces them.

Problems can arise in any area of life and may be seemingly trivial, e.g. where do you go on a Friday night, or more weighty, what do you do if your landlord informs you in the middle of the year that s/he is selling the house that you live in? Some problems may be similar to ones you have encountered before, and therefore you may have previous knowledge or experience to help you. Others may be completely novel, so requiring new approaches.

This section aims to provide a general framework or model which individuals and groups can follow in attempting to solve problems that they may face. Although this framework will be presented as a series of independent steps which individuals or groups take when solving problems, it is possible that the various stages of the process may be difficult to separate out in practice. It is hoped, however, that this framework will provide a basis for you to achieve more effective problem solving.

CONTENTS

This section presents the stages to be followed in solving problems. These will be illustrated with examples which should help to clarify the points raised, and then a worked example will be presented.

HOW TO USE 'SIMPLE SOLUTIONS'

Like any such techniques concerned with doing things better or more efficiently, problem-solving techniques need to be practised until they become a natural component of your problem solving. It may be useful, therefore, each time you encounter a problem to refer back to the following framework until the process becomes automatic.

THE PROBLEM-SOLVING PROCESS[1]

The first stage in solving any problem is **PROBLEM IDENTIFICATION**. This simply means recognising that a problem exists.

---

1. Based on K. Wexley and L. Yukl, *Organizational Behavior and Personnel Psychology* (Illinois: Richard D. Irwin, 1984).

5. Simple Solutions

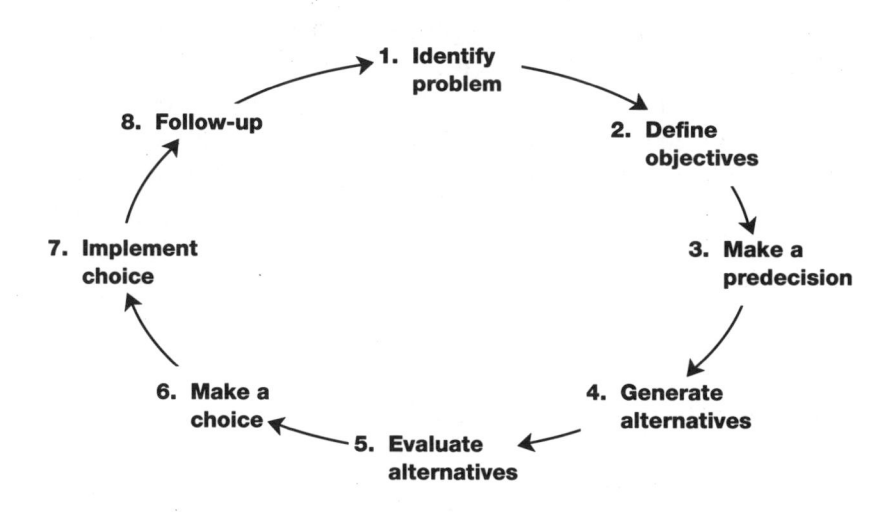

1. Identify problem
2. Define objectives
3. Make a predecision
4. Generate alternatives
5. Evaluate alternatives
6. Make a choice
7. Implement choice
8. Follow-up

This may seem trivial; however, within this stage it is very important that you spend time to **CLARIFY THE PROBLEM** and to define it. One of the many ways in which the mind attempts to make life easier is to solve the first impression of the problem that it encounters. Thus as human beings we have a tendency to pick the most obvious shortcoming in any problem situation and set to work on it. Not considering the problem fully at this stage may

CLARIFY THE PROBLEM BEFORE TRYING TO SOLVE IT!

Successful Study

result in problems at later stages, or it may mean that the original problem remains unsolved. For example, you may increase the number of references that you include in your essays to increase your marks, only to find what is causing your low marks (the problem) was your writing style and not the number of references you used. It is therefore important that you consider fully any problem you encounter before attempting to solve it and think carefully about its causes. You may find it useful to try to communicate your problem to someone else, as in doing so you may end up with a clearer or different view of it.

Once the problem has been identified and clarified, the next stage is to **DEFINE THE OBJECTIVES TO BE MET IN SOLVING THE PROBLEM**. If you decide what your aims are in solving the problem, then when you consider possible solutions you can compare these with your objectives. If the problem is that someone in your house is using your milk, the objective in solving the problem may be to stop this person using what belongs to you, but to do this without creating any bad feelings.

Once you have decided what you want to achieve, the next stage in the process is to **MAKE A PREDECISION**. This simply means

GENERATE ALTERNATIVES

5. Simple Solutions

BRAINSTORMING

deciding how to make the decision about what to do. You may want to solve the problem on your own without consulting other people, or you may want to ask for the opinions of others and consider these when you make your decision. Alternatively, the problem may be one which has been given to a group, therefore a group decision will be needed.

Once you have clarified the problem, defined your aims for solving it and decided how you are going to make your decision, it is time to **GENERATE ALTERNATIVES**, or identify possible solutions to the problem. This is one area where most people spend too little time and do not explore a wide enough range of alternative solutions.

To generate solutions to problems, you may rely on approaches you have previously used. These may provide ready-made answers if similar problems have been encountered before.

If the problem is new, you should generate as many alternative solutions as possible. A useful technique for doing this is called **'brainstorming'**. *Brainstorming involves writing down as many potential solutions as you can on a piece of paper. You should concentrate on generating as many*

Successful Study

solutions as you can and suspend judgement about how feasible they are until you have thought of as many as you can.

All of the solutions which you generate to a problem may not be equally feasible. The next stage, therefore, in problem solving is to **EVALUATE ALTERNATIVE SOLUTIONS**. This involves deciding which solution would be most effective in reaching the objectives identified in the second stage of the framework. In the example of someone using your milk, possible alternatives may be to:

- ▼ Leave a note on the fridge door asking whoever it is to stop;
- ▼ Hide your milk elsewhere; or
- ▼ Approach the person and discuss the problem with him/her.

As the objective was to stop this person using what belongs to you without creating bad feeling, the third option may be most appropriate. The first may generate animosity and the second is impractical since it would mean keeping your milk outside the fridge.

5. Simple Solutions

The next step involves making a **CHOICE**. This is essential in solving any problem. After several alternatives have been evaluated, the one that is considered most acceptable is chosen. In the milk example, this would be to approach the person and discuss the problem with him/her. In doing this, the seventh stage in solving a problem would be fulfilled, i.e. **IMPLEMENTING THE CHOSEN SOLUTION**, or carrying out the course of action you have chosen to solve the problem.

Finally, it is important that you **FOLLOW UP** any decisions you have made and consider whether you have effectively solved the problem. Does it still exist or has your course of action led to any new problems? If it has, you will need to begin the process again.

THE PROBLEM-SOLVING PROCESS
An Illustrated Example

Description of the problem

On successful completion of your exams you proceed to the final year of your course. As a final-year student you are required to choose the courses you will take.

Having chosen your six options and started to really enjoy your course, you are presented with a piece of course work you just have no idea how to complete. Further to this, this piece of work is a part of your last choice option which you really didn't want to do. Consequently, you feel at a loss, doubting your own abilities, and your option choices, and generally feeling confused. However, you soon realise that this is a problem that needs to be solved, so what do you do?

Successful Study

1. Identify problem

You realise that in order to solve this problem you must first identify exactly what you find difficult — what is the cause of the problem. You may ask yourself questions:

- Do I lack the necessary intelligence?
- Have I not done enough preparatory reading?
- Am I just bored with the subject?
- Does this piece of work follow on from previous work I missed?
- Perhaps my idea of hard work is inappropriate and I just need to try harder.
- Is there some key issue or concept concerning this work that I have failed to grasp?

After asking yourself these questions you realise that several of the above might be valid. You acknowledge that you did not work very hard last year and may have missed several relevant lectures, but you doubt you lack the intelligence. You identify the problem as a lack of previous knowledge adding to a conceptually difficult problem making progress seem impossible.

2. Define objectives

In order to set about solving the problem you decide to set yourself some objectives. You decide that what you want most is to eliminate the negative emotions you feel, and to do this you must complete the piece of work satisfactorily.

3. Make a predecision

Next you need to decide how you are going to solve the problem. At this stage you need to make a few preliminary decisions. How do you feel about other people knowing about your difficulties? Are you prepared to accept help from others? Or, do you feel this is

5. Simple Solutions

something you have to accomplish alone? You decide that the most important thing is to complete the piece of work and that any help will be appreciated.

4. Generate alternatives

Although you have at this stage thought about overcoming the problem, you have yet to decide exactly how you will attempt to solve it. You think of as many possible solutions as you can. These might include:

- ▼ Leaving your course.
- ▼ Speaking to a lecturer.
- ▼ Asking a friend to explain it.
- ▼ Copying from a friend.
- ▼ Attempting to cover the background work quickly.

5. Evaluate alternatives

Faced with numerous possibilities you imagine carrying out each and what the results would be, and compare these to your objectives. Leaving your course would alleviate the necessity to complete the work, but would only increase feelings of incompetence. Cheating would satisfy your tutor, but not yourself. Seeking help and at the same time covering missed work on the other hand might lead to completion of the work and a satisfactory feeling about yourself.

6. Make a choice

You select the solution which you consider most likely to meet your objectives — to ask a friend to explain the background work and then to get help from a lecturer if necessary, and to put a bit of effort in.

7. Implement choice

You consult a friend, copy missed lecture notes, get an explanation of the conceptual difficulties from your tutor and set about completing the work in question.

8. Follow up

On completion of the task you assess your current state of affairs and establish whether your objectives have been met.

IMPORTANT POINTS TO REMEMBER

▼ Make sure you clarify the problem before attempting to solve it.

▼ Generate a range of alternative solutions — the most obvious solution is not necessarily the best.

▼ Follow up your decisions — have you successfully solved the problem?

6
PAINLESS PRESENTATIONS

THIS SECTION is designed for people who have little or no knowledge of how to do a formal, verbal presentation. It does not aim to turn you into the world's best public speaker in quarter of an hour. Instead, by providing you with a framework within which you can work while developing your own presentation style, it will hopefully give you the confidence to stand up and 'have a go'. It also includes a means to assess your presentations yourself, or to have others assess them constructively, to help you focus your development.

CONTENTS

'Painless Presentations' contains guidance notes on how to do a verbal presentation, a 'Painless Presentations' preparation checklist and a 'Painless Presentations' assessment sheet. The preparation checklist is a summary of the main points discussed in the guidance notes and should be used when you are planning and constructing your presentation. The assessment sheet allows you to rate the individual components of a presentation, outlined in the checklist and the notes, as well as the overall impression that the presenter gave.

Successful Study

HOW TO USE 'PAINLESS PRESENTATIONS'

The contents of this section should be used as a personal learning tool. It is in no way definitive, nor is it meant to be. It has been designed to provide a sensible basis for developing your own presentation styles, adding or deleting as you see fit.

The guidance notes should be read before you start to plan your presentation.

The checklist, on its own, can be used as preparation for your own presentation or to help others prepare for theirs.

The assessment sheet can be used to rate both yourself and other presenters, either formally or informally. You can either rate yourself after each presentation and watch how your style develops, or you can ask members of your audience to rate you. The assessment sheet can help you to focus on the individual components of a presentation, either to look at other people's techniques that you would like to develop, or to provide a basis for providing constructive criticism of a presentation.

6. Painless Presentations

GUIDANCE NOTES

Introduction

Conventional wisdom rightly says that thorough preparation makes a successful presentation. What conventional wisdom fails to say, and this section aims to address, is what you must actually prepare.

There are four basic factors that will affect the overall impression you give to an audience when you are presenting. These are the structure and content of your talk, your style of delivery, your use of visual aids and your handling of questions. We'll focus on each of these factors in turn. First, however, before starting to look at these factors, it is important to do a little groundwork.

Before starting to develop your presentation it is important to ask yourself a number of questions.

- ▼ What is the aim of your talk? Is it to inform, to persuade, to amuse?

- ▼ What are the key points you want to get across to your audience? How long have you got to make them?

- ▼ Who are your audience? How many of them are there?

- ▼ What do they know about your subject?

The answers to these questions will determine what you do in the next four sections.

BE PREPARED!

Structure

All presentations should have a beginning, a middle and an end. At the beginning you should say what you are about to say, in the middle you should say it, and at the end you should tell the audience what you have just said. It may be old advice but it makes for effective presentations.

Your opening, or introduction, should include an outline of what will be covered in your presentation and the structure you will follow. It should also put the content of the talk into some context. This is particularly important for an audience who do not have much knowledge of your subject area. Finally, your opening should include the objectives of your presentation (to inform, to persuade, or to amuse?).

The main body of your presentation should develop logically. Points should be made clearly and 'signposted' by phrases such as 'What I have just described illustrates . . .', or 'From this it is clear that . . .'. When changing subjects and moving on to make new points, linkage should be clear. The audience should be made aware that the presenter has finished talking about subject A and is now talking about subject B. For example: 'I have just made the point that . . . , now let us move on to . . .'.

When closing a presentation, the main points you have made should be briefly summarised, i.e. 'telling the audience what you have told them'. It is important that you finish your presentation cleanly, rather than drifting off to an indefinite end. This should be done with a concluding sentence or two, related to the objectives you stated at the beginning. For example, 'What I hope to have achieved this morning, through discussing these points . . . , is to have shown that . . .'

Delivery

No matter how good the structure of your talk is, the way you put it across to your audience is of key importance

6. Painless Presentations

to the impression you will give to them. Preparation, again, is important.

You should have rehearsed and should know your presentation well enough to use prompt cards (small cards with key points or phrases on them to prompt you) only, rather than reading your presentation from A4 sheets of paper.

As you are presenting to an audience, look at the audience. Don't look at the floor, the ceiling, the back wall, or, importantly, the overhead projector screen. Look at the audience!

Speak clearly, varying the pace and rhythm of your speech somewhat, to maintain the interest of your viewers. Importantly, use language appropriate to your audience, don't talk up or down to them. This is particularly important when presenting technical material to 'non-technical' people.

Choose before you speak — based on the room and audience size — whether you are going to sit or stand. If you are giving your presentation standing up, move around a little to help keep your audience interested. Use appropriate gestures to help illustrate what you are saying. Whichever you choose, try to appear comfortable and natural, even if you don't feel it.

Successful Study

Nearly everybody feels nervous when doing presentations. Practising your presentation beforehand helps considerably. It is also helpful to become familiar with the idea of doing presentations by actually doing as many as you can. All of this doesn't seem to help much when you have to do one for your first time, though.

Remember that the audience is generally on your side and wants to see you do well. Mistakes you make that you think are enormous are probably not even noticed by an audience. If you do make a large mistake or lose track of what you are doing, as everybody does at some time, stop. Look at your notes, get your bearings, take a deep breath to relax, and carry on.

Nobody expects your presentation to be perfect.

6. Painless Presentations

Practise using the visual aids you have chosen, beforehand, so that you know what you are doing during the presentation. Always turn off the overhead or slide projector when you are not actively using it. When drawing the audience's attention to a particular point on an overhead transparency, point on the transparency itself and not on the screen.

If you have a time limit for your talk, make sure that you stick to it. Don't go on for too long, or stop too soon.

Visual aids

Visual aids are used to help convey ideas and information in a way that they are more easily understood.

There are a number of visual aids available to presenters. These include overhead transparencies, boards, flip charts, slides, models, etc. It is important to remember that visual aids exist to support the spoken component of the presentation and should only be used when they **add** to what is said. They should fit well with the talk, illustrating and highlighting points as necessary.

Work out beforehand exactly what you want from a particular visual and think about other ways of presenting the same information. Instead of tables of figures (Table 1), perhaps you could use a graph (Figure 1). Make it as simple and as bold as possible. Too

	1	2	3	4	5	6
A	25	60	70	75	80	81
B	35	45	55	60	65	70
C	35	35	40	40	35	30
D	30	30	30	25	25	25
E	70	65	60	55	50	45

Table 1: *Change in percentage over time by group*

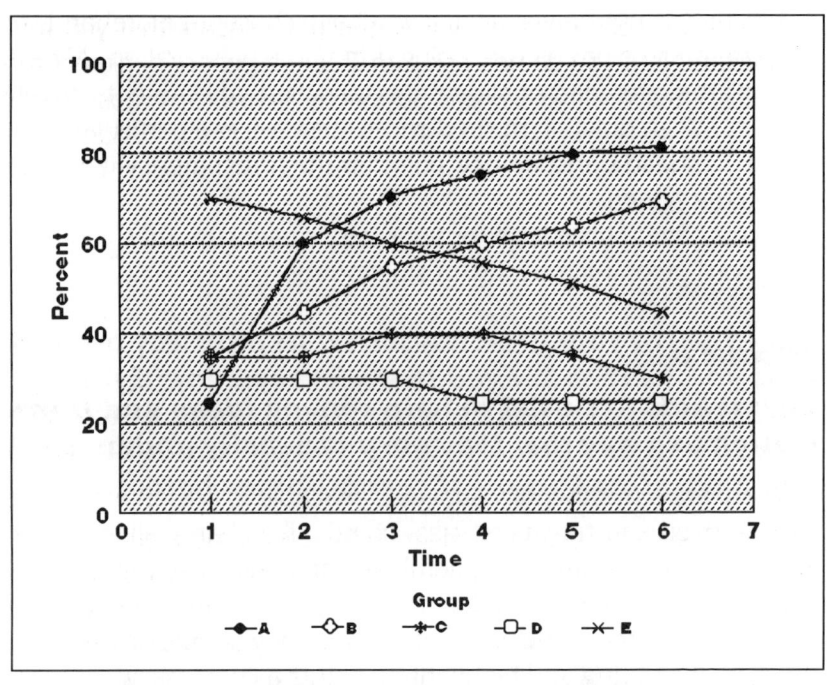

Figure 1: *Change in percentage over time by group*

much information on one visual aid makes it difficult for the audience to read. Try to make your visual aids as interesting as possible.

Question handling

Here your audience have an opportunity to participate, developing their understanding of what you have said, and indirectly, testing yours. Your presentation is not over yet! It is important that you know what you are talking about.

Let your audience know at the beginning when you want to receive questions. Some people like to field questions during the presentation, others at the end. It is up to you — it is your presentation. If someone asks a question during your presentation and you are not ready to answer it, tell them so and that you will come back to that point at the end of the talk.

6. Painless Presentations

When someone does ask you a question, ensure that you fully understand it. If you do not, ask him/her to repeat or explain it further, then answer it clearly and succinctly. If you can't, it is usually safer to say so than to try to bluff or waffle your way through, particularly when you are presenting to an audience with some knowledge of your subject.

Summary

Rehearsal of your presentation is the only way to check that you have managed to get everything right. You will also be pleasantly surprised at how much better you will feel actually doing the presentation when you have already done it several times before.

These notes are only a guide to help you do more effective presentations. As you get more experience, you should try doing things in different ways and develop your own style of presentation. Remember, it is important that you feel comfortable with what you are doing!

PREPARATION CHECKLIST

Is your presentation right for your audience, room size and objectives and the time available?

Structure

- ▼ Does your **OPENING** contain an outline of the talk, set the context and state your objectives?
- ▼ What are the main points you want to make?
- ▼ Do they follow each other logically, linking together well?
- ▼ Are they well 'signposted', covering the material you want to cover?

Successful Study

- Do they need support from visual aids?
- When **CLOSING** do you sum up the main points and make a strong conclusion?

Delivery

- Do you know your presentation? Are you going to talk from cards?
- Are you going to sit or stand?
- Who are you going to look at?
- Is the language you are going to use right for your audience?
- Do you know how to use your visual aids?

Visual aids

- Are your visual aids simple, interesting and easy to read?
- Do they fit well with your talk and **add** to your presentation?

Question handling

- Do you know what you are talking about?
- Can you anticipate and prepare for any likely questions?
- Do you think you can answer clearly any relevant questions?
- **How do you know the answers to these questions? Have you practised?**

PRESENTATION ASSESSMENT SHEET

▬ PRESENTER:

▬ STRUCTURE OF TALK:

Opening	Poor introduction. No outline	1 2 3 4 5	Good introduction and outline of presentation
Sequencing of material	Poor sequencing and linkage	1 2 3 4 5	Good sequencing — well linked
Coverage of material	Poor coverage of subject area. Main points not clearly 'signposted'	1 2 3 4 5	Subject area well covered. Clear 'signposting' of main points
Closing	Poor summary of content	1 2 3 4 5	Good summary of content

▬ DELIVERY:

Appearance	Appears poorly prepared	1 2 3 4 5	Appears well prepared
Voice clarity	Monotonous and unclear	1 2 3 4 5	Varied speed and flow of speech, easy to understand
Stance/gestures	Appears nervous and uncomfortable, few gestures	1 2 3 4 5	Appears confident and comfortable, appropriate gestures
Eye contact with audience	Poor/inappropriate	1 2 3 4 5	Good/appropriate
Handling of audience	Talked up/down to audience	1 2 3 4 5	Appropriate level of speech for audience. Effective use of participation
Handling of visual aids	Poor/inappropriate	1 2 3 4 5	Effective/appropriate
Timing	Too long/short	1 2 3 4 5	Well timed to meet time limit

▬ VISUAL AIDS:

Quality	Poorly prepared, hard to read	1 2 3 4 5	Well prepared, easy to read
Suitability	Do not fit well with talk	1 2 3 4 5	Fitted well with talk

▬ QUESTION HANDLING:

Knowledge of subject	Poor knowledge of subject	1 2 3 4 5	Good knowledge of subject
Clarity and relevance of answers	Questions poorly answered	1 2 3 4 5	Questions well answered

▬ GENERAL IMPRESSION:

	Very poor	1 2 3 4 5	Excellent

▬ COMMENTS: